THE FREQUENCY OF LIFE

A Collection of Word Art and Artwork

KARI BEYER

Copyright © 2020 Kari Beyer
Cover Design: @vanessarnaynard
Published by: Big Moose Publishing
PO Box 127 Site 601 RR#6 Saskatoon, SK CANADA S7K3J9
www.bigmoosepublishing.com

All rights reserved. No part of this book may be used or reproduced by any means, graphic, electronic, or mechanical, including photocopying, recording, taping or by any information storage retrieval system without the written permission of the author except in the case of brief quotations embodied in critical articles and reviews.

Because of the dynamic nature of the Internet, any web addresses or links contained in this book may have changed since publication and may no longer be valid. The views expressed in this work are solely those of the author(s) and do not necessarily reflect the views of the publisher, and the publisher hereby disclaims any responsibility for them.

The author(s) of this book does not dispense medical advice or prescribe the use of any technique as a form of treatment for physical, emotional, or medical problems without the advice of a physician, either directly or indirectly. The intent of the author is only to offer information of a general nature to help you in your quest for emotional and spiritual well-being. In the event you use any of the information in this book for yourself, which is your constitutional right, the author and the publisher assume no responsibility for your actions.

ISBN: 978-1-989840-03-0 (paperback)
ISBN: 978-1-989840-04-7 (e-book)

Big Moose Publishing 3/2020

For all who need love and support on their journey, this book is for you where you are - accepting, observing your experiences and loving yourself more fully.

CONTENTS

ACKNOWLEDGMENTS ix
INTRODUCTION xi
Heart Wisdom 1
Water Marigold Fairy Garden 4
Sparkle and Shine 5
Overture 8
Loving Breath 10
Daily Wanderings 12
Sacred Space 14
comfort 15
Lost Lover 18
Searching Back 21
Hidden Spirit 24
Relaxed Expansion 25
Blame Throwing 27
Explosions...Incoming Masculine 30
Life Force- Expanding 31
No Barriers 34
Fire Raging 37
Pulling Me In 40
The Enemy Within 41
The Way 43
A Center 46
Interrupt 49
Advanced Exposure 52
Cryptic Memories 53
Flicking 56
Fresh New Fruit 57
Gentle Horizons 60
Falling Down 63

Nourishment 65
High Speed Femininity 66
Hook Handle 69
One Step at a Time 72
Busy 75
Tree of Oneness and Now 78
Eradicated Version 79
Rampant Deforestation 82
Hot and Cold 84
The Big Picture 87
Discovery 90
Dust Blown 91
Dumping Ground 94
Focus Changer 96
Self-Speak 98
Hiding Within 101
This is Mine 102
Circling 104
New Directions 107
Water Rising 109
Dragons 112
Generational Journey 113
The Old Cold Masculine 116
Shitty Days 118
Being Elsewhere 121
Restricted Energies 123
Fun 126
Protocol of Niceness Part 1 129
Much More Balance 132
The Protocol of Niceness Part 2 133
Three Thoughts to Hope 135
Heart of a Woman 139
Epilogue 140
Uncovering 143
Who I Am 145

Finite Wonder	148
Personal	149
Mom and Me	149
Mounting Blue	152
Sexy	155
Satifsied	156
Loving Me	159
ABOUT THE AUTHOR	161
INDEX	162

ACKNOWLEDGMENTS

Thank you to all that have been on and helped me on my journey. There are too many to name.

To my partner in life and love, Greg, thank you for your honesty and support always.

Brin, Simon and Ruby thank you for trusting me to take care of you. I am glad you are flying.

Mom and Dad, thank you for this new relationship.

Gloria Stefanson, thank you for being you and sharing your gift with me.

Katie Bell thank you for your pushes!

Vicki Page, thank you for your love and support.

Breyann Pollard, thank you for making sense of my writing.

If we have had a relationship, you have helped me grow. Thank you.

INTRODUCTION

The journey to my heart has been a long one. Every experience scratching the surface a little bit more. Pushing the limits of change has me seeing my heart bursting open. These big changes make it possible for me to see myself a little clearer, with more moments without pain, stress, and overreactions.

This word art and art work have been composed to bring healing to all who observe them. Words and art have different affects on people. For example, if I said brown banana you each may have a different story for those words. Each shape may look different to each person. One shape may look like a smile to one person but a wave to another. With all of these observations there is a lot of emotion that comes up too. These words and art pieces are created to work on many levels. The words can be read many times with different meanings or a new outlook from the first to last time.

These compositions can be read as an entire collection or individually. It took me over a year to read the whole collection at once, so pace yourself.

As you read, observe, or listen to the words and art pieces make sure to:

1. Give yourself the space to look inward. See what emotions, memories, attitudes, or places these individual pieces bring up. If you would like to see how I use words and art then look at the back of the book under Personal for examples. This is only one way to do it. Enjoy your own process.

2. Take breaks and breathe when you are feeling stuck, have emotions come up, or need to let the words filter into you. Observe how you feel with no judgement.

3. When choosing an individual page or pages, trust your intuition; flip to a page and read.

4. These words and art are for you. I have written and painted them with the intent for them to be for all who observe them. This does not mean they are for you every day, or perhaps they are.

5. Read these words at different times in your life. You may see different meanings or receive different insights, depending on your frame of mind or how you have grown.

Possibilities:

- Write your observations down. Writing your first reaction is usually the most authentic. Try not to think about what you write.

- Reading the poetry and looking at the art pieces

together will add another dimension. I have suggestions, but the art could go with any of the poems. One painting may go with many poems or many paintings can go with one poem.

- Read aloud, or have someone read the words to you. Experience.

- There are questions. You can answer them or not. Open ended questions help your body, too.

- Make your own art piece.

- Book a healing session to dig deeper.

The paintings can be observed in different ways. Here are some suggestions:

1. When looking at a painting the first question is "which way is up?" Turn it the right way for you.

2. What do you see?

3. Put the art work where you can observe it. See if it changes.

4. Repeat steps 1&2 whenever you notice it again.

Healing comes in all forms. This form comes out of pain, my love for poetry, art, mindscape, and also from the idea that we all need a gentle universal way to heal. We are all perfectly made. The knowledge that healing can be flowing through words, art, moments of breathing and grace can bring us all to a different mindset and let the healing take place.

Gentle healing does not mean that you won't find moments of hardship. Give yourself the space you need to allow for your body mind to readjust. Our mind is a powerful tool- your physical and mental body may need gentleness, support and space to catch up to your heart.

There is also the aspect of frequency. Words, colours and shapes all have frequency. White light goes into a prism and the rainbow comes out. This is measurable. Our voices have frequencies that are measurable too. Our body sends off frequencies as well. We draw people to us who possess matching or opposite frequencies. We are drawn to our jobs, houses, our friends, music, and many more. Sometimes these relationships between us and other humans, animals and things bring us stress and pain because of the frequencies and in spite of them. This book is written and art composed to deliver you healing frequencies of love, observation and gratitude. These frequencies can help your body heal, align and reconnect.

From the ages of 0-7 we make a fundamental set of beliefs. These beliefs have helped us to survive and keep us safe. They were made from the perspective of our younger self and a lot of them are emotional and limiting. They are causing us pain and stress. In having these limiting beliefs we attract our jobs, houses, possessions, friends, money, music, etc. These things, experiences and people contain a message to help us to break apart our limiting beliefs and allow us to become less emotional about our decisions. Making decisions from our child-like beliefs can be very emotional. In reading this book, choosing healing and self-care you are making the decision to heal those beliefs that have been limiting you and give yourself the ability to make choices from a place of wisdom and acting in the present moment, not the past.

Our world and body are constantly giving us clues to help us heal. They want us to get the picture. If we do not they repeat the message again and again. Instead of fighting it what if we embraced these messages and turned them into wisdom?

Our body knows better than our mind. This is why they pair so well together. Sometimes this healing is better to do when our conscious mind is confused or busy. That is why these words and breathing through them is so important.

May this book help you along your own path of healing and self-reflection. Your body knows what it needs to heal itself. Trust it!

Heart Wisdom

Right inside the wisdom of the heart comes

a deep Jagged sense of knowing

That aches in the legs

Unsure it can carry the weight of the knowing

unsure of being enough.

    How wretched is this unstirring,

Loosened from the path of ok

Wandering the halls of worry,

Bringing fluffs of baggage

    Unable to take the many optional doorways

        Skylights to other universes

        This path is carved out from many

        hallway wanderings.

            Size grown to fit the caverness way

taking smaller pathways may not fit

For what may great extension take

Do we have patience to sit and wait in the silence to hear the nattering's of our hearts?

It is calling, wanting to burst through revealing the past hurts, traumas, and those belief systems that are no longer needed.

My heart is waiting for me to reveal itself. To crack open the hard shell that holds it back, revealing so many colours, options, possibilities flowing out so it cannot stop.

THE FREQUENCY OF LIFE

What are your possibilities?
~Write or draw your thoughts here~

"Water Marigold Fairy Garden"

Sparkle and Shine

As we hit the pavement of our life

Dullness seeps through our existence

Generating energy that we cannot do without

Suffering seems safer than the unachievable

Sparkle that we see around us.

The stench of pain surrounds us and has us

Breathe it in, through our pours and our existence

The suffering goes on.

The path to seeing a way out is the longest.

Once we have this mission accomplished there are so many

Ways out. Our exit strategy has so many wormholes

We are our worst enemy.

How do we see the enemy is us, not others, not something

else that we don't have control of-

We need those things to keep us in this darkness.

The sparkle and shine is the hardest to see in me

Accepting the good- the bright, the brilliant-

Making my teeth hurt with the sweetness.

Can we bite into that delicious love of self

with ease and satisfaction?

A warm hug comes in our sorrow

Having us turn back to the pain once more

The knowledge of our progress is out of our reach until

We can self-reflect. Without the pain

in the spring of our healing.

Sometimes our spirit suffers and takes the brunt of our struggles. How has your spirit been the opposite of sparkle and shine?

Are there ways to not ignore or give negative attention to your spirit? Or are there ways to give positive attention to your spirit?

Are there ways to put you first?

~Write or draw your thoughts here~

Overture

Palm on Face

Knot in stomach

Using head instead of Heart

The life vessel of the gut bring Robin's song shrill and high

Morning sun has high reflective properties

Spilling in my front window diffused by

curtains capturing the branches beauty.

Nurture

All these signs around us capture the essence of me. They are here to show me the beauty of me. Sometimes they feel like "why is this happening to me?" But the message is showing you where you came from, what your battles are, and how to open up for what is to come.

What are you noticing today? Is there a repeating message?

~Write or draw your thoughts here~

Loving Breath

Breathe into this awkwardness of living.

As we get used to breathing into the uncomfortable duality we can open up to many more awkward breathings.

Have you been excited for the next awkward breathing?

What if this awkwardness could bring us to a huge revelation? And what if this also could help us love more? Be more? Create more?

Could you feel excited then? See if you can just breathe into this awkwardness. If the only thing you could do is love yourself right now, would you?

~Write or draw your thoughts here~

Daily Wanderings

Outside noise distracts our daily wanderings

How favorable our noise could be if we only

kept our focus inward-skybattle as we

thrash ourselves for our bad behavior.

But our path needs to lead us here; if not...our wanderings
    could not have us

back home, at rest, puzzle fitting, figuring our own path of
healing,

unique to only me.

What if your wanderings- mentally, physically, spiritually, or emotionally- were where you were "supposed to be?"

What would your reality be now?

~Write or draw your thoughts here~

"Sacred Space"

comfort

mixing, mashing
sun filtered soft and lazy
Dynamic hot/cold, Bright shadow
All has us unaware of the possibility.
Finding ease instead of mushiness
brings definition.
    Masses moving gut wrench,
ancestral lands fought out for the reverence
hidden shadows tell us other stories of long forgotten
mysteries
unhinging mysteries can bring us peace and ease.
without dragging us through obligatory adding of
words without meaning or sense.
    Senses have brought us here,
to this place of now.

Kari Beyer

How overcome with sense we can be.

Who or what has influenced our

sense of decency our

cents of value our

scents of humanity-

Are we not the observer of all feeling, gained in our world?

How do we influence our own senses?

Our senses are what we base our reality on. When we were brought into this world we came from safety and needed to create safety in our world. We had to make rules that would keep us safe.

For example, if we touched something hot we would know not to touch it anymore.

Sometimes what kept us safe as a child is no longer safe now, but we still have the limiting belief. What if we could observe without rules? What would our senses say?

~Write or draw your thoughts here~

Lost Lover

I feel like a long lost lover

Waiting to open the secret heart that I didn't know was there.

The other side unsure- frustrated

With the naivety that was always there.

As information has been acquired the

thrilled sound pulls heart strings down

to guide deeper. Breath taken

discernment required to reach too deep in the gut of making concrete.

the knowledge of unsurpassed judgements.

That have been a part of the history

 a part of the gates that held back a strong determined goddess

a force and nature

      Rapture... as in claiming the scraps at the end to take

with

how much more real can you be- more rational does not make sense anymore-

waiting for the nod could take forever unless we nod to ourselves first.

How do we ok us, our feminine nature?

Can we help it to be rooted, stable?

or do we need the change that comes to be fluid, always Changing?

like the breeze so we can see the other side as it flips and changes with every light, every new idea, every new discovery

How many faces do we have?

As we change do we have more?

      The face of bitterness can be a season or

a friend that comes by to visit in passing time.

When it says hell low how do we greet it?

The same each time?

Can we switch, then move it, change it-

Give it an exit strategy?

      Like a newly formed bud waiting for its potential.

This wealth of energy has formed for beauty

Kari Beyer

~Write or draw your thoughts here~

Searching Back

Looking, searching back

To a time before when there was no interruption

No experience, no skills... how long did I

Search for those things.

Longing for it to start and as I pass the years by I glimpse back with careful eyes to see what has passed-

curiosity but with a careful glance unsure if it is what I want to see

As emotions rise from old memories

The door closes, so unforgotten past can sit in silence a bit longer.

Building me up to strength again

Maybe this time will be easier-

Maybe I can see more or handle it longer

The old pain.

Commitment to the project- self commitment of a new kind

makes it easier/harder to see that phase of life.

Self-commitment such strange words

For my eyes see this in too many lights-

Ignoring, tuning out, with disregard,

angrily...

but past that as I feel this pain an echo of the old soul the self before the pain peeks through and sighs.

Hope for another tomorrow.

What are your dreams?

Have they changed?

~Write or draw your thoughts here~

"Hidden Spirit"

Relaxed Expansion

As I sit here I feel like stretching back and having a smoke. It feels like an after dinner cigarette.

This is a moment when I have a feeling of pride, satisfaction and expansion of the heart and lungs.

This feeling I need more of. The space I create in these moments gives my body a curve that I am able to accelerate into. Possibilities created, my launching point usually has me bending forward. What if my launch was to receive (rather than in the ready position) in a more relaxed expansion, pride and satisfaction?

So much stands in my way of launching or so I make myself believe.

Little specks in the forefront of my vision- they distract me from the big picture.

That amazing feeling comes out of something that is looked down on. Here is a nugget of treasure.

Kari Beyer

What kind of life would we lead if we were not worried what people thought?

~Write or draw your thoughts here~

Blame Throwing

Inanimate object

Caught up, controlled by generous life force

Do we like to be here acting as insignificant as we do? Why Blame throw?

Choking on words that cannot be said or said too much,

looking down on curly innocence

To be taken over- power controlled or not

Choice given- decisions unmade- made for you?

No- Choice is always there

    Why not take back the action of throwing,

in order to dissolve the circular game

    that never ends- once a player

    Finds ways to unveil- coward hidden

No longer necessary - For label throwing past necessity no longer -

    Creeping up on vulnerability could result in

reactionary means -

but when met with adaptation

can resolve large conflict

bringing fruits of Beauty

~Write or draw your thoughts here~

"Explosions...Incoming Masculine"

Life Force- Expanding

I feel my cells changing rearranging

To placid memories of before

    The fall-

leaves me petaling towards the suspended wave.

Previous experience wanders close to great knowledge of what's to follow.

    Is that always- unpredictability

Flourishes in the right game- did you sign up?

How do I know the game is even signable

Lost branches are they missed?

    By robin's nest- unknown paths taken.

Was the tree here and rooted before? Was it meant to grow lost branches?

    Without, am I longing? Missing- like an amputee feeling for lost limbs-

Afraid of similarities to octopuses

Kari Beyer

Growing back arms are too cumbersome

Giving space for shining,

Giving space for what is as important as disappearing limbs

To show trueness,

glory Life Force expanding.

~Write or draw your thoughts here~

No Barriers

Un-pedaled sun

      Soft and deeply absorbs the warm

Mellows rags that enter me as though there were no barriers

Fight through the barrier as we drag the limp limb along.

Fighting for time, distance, strength

Locked limbs stretching, pulling

A new way gives different fruit?

Foreign concept off the distant land

Not here.

Still trying old ways for new results,

Seems insane

Yet trial seems the only way.

Options are crushed by options

Instincts take over-

Before you know it

Foreign words come out never heard before.

A rarity,

Stiff upper lip seems to take emotion on-

Scaled invaders

One puff of hope

Whoa-

This is possible?...!

Realization the world will not end

If new actions are taken to

replace not drown out old necessities

Space needed-

And given with new openings

Kari Beyer

How long have you been forcing yourself to take it? Be stronger, work harder, and keep pushing along. What if you gave you space, to be creative, to be open to new possibilities, to let yourself unwind?

~Write or draw your thoughts here~

Fire Raging

As cold rain drops quell the burning need to explode

Turning, changing

Still not ready-emotions fizzle

As fire cools internal flame waiting

For a breath to rise again.

      Fuel, oxygen, heat

Are required but other options?

A face looks over into the abyss

As light stares above

Idea…

Possibilities register as waves of heat arise.

Shifting,

Lost as a bug in the great unknown

Closing up the spilling of too many unrequited memories-

Soft fusion of this new dimension of awareness

Is anyone here?

Fear- This new reality is missing its teams of leaders/followers-line mates.

No hints on what, where, how, when, why?

How to navigate? Who to be? Where to go? What to do? Why…?

~Write or draw your thoughts here~

"Pulling Me In"

The Enemy Within

Come to me

A soft breath is saying come to me-

Rejection is running rampant- the foreign concept of mirroring him my masculine to get my entry point

How much have I given to get to here?

Now you have to enter realms of the enemy- where old pictures are at every turn-

That house

Brings me back to my knees

The pity, the anguish, stripped bare

      Knowledge of unforeseen deities lies in his hands-

It makes sense to me-

Why do I have to play games? It is already known- and each layer is there an end?

How minute are the dreams- when stopped by a giant that you are riding on his back, is he holding your dreams?

Kari Beyer

~Write or draw your thoughts here~

The Way

A small noise overhead has us drawn back to our idea-

The possibility

Stripped bare feeling shaky in my knees

The science overwhelms.

As old angers

Glimmer on the edge of this step.

To go along with others- back to before would be so easy-

No ridicule, no waves rocking my inner equilibrium

Vines reaching into nothing

Looking frayed, miss kept for hoping there is another option.

Exit strategy in place

Hard work expels beads of sweat, emotions released so that staring into abyss can be avoided again, until it builds again.

The rock needs to be shovelled around, pried out, cut in to pieces to be more manageable

That will do the trick.

How many times do we wish away our now?

Wish for a big project done.

Hope that our time goes quicker.

If we could only not be alone,

If we could only be alone,

We wish to be older, wish to be younger, or wish to be anything than what we are now.

What if the now was all that we had?

Why are we so uncomfortable in this moment?

Some questions may beg to be answered, but some questions can be left open, to contemplate. Maybe you are not the one that needs to answer them. The answer may come organically.

~Write or draw your thoughts here~

A Center

The picture within a picture

Memories of long ago, battles won become a glossy form of their once forgotten memory.

   A deceit

Thunder rolls in

   Pop, crack- the arrow hits the target, practice again.
Pop crack

The sound around uninterrupted correction, correction made-

Rumble

Birds continue their mating song.

Stay the course

Pop Crack-

Louder still

Moaning thunder repeats its low growl.

The entire orchestra fits in toon

Driven by purpose- what purpose is this?

Who is drawing my tune?

     The bare waves of long ago carve a path of unmistakable weight

Smoking out intruders that have left their mark

Floating above all this a wispy thought emerges of reality.

Is any of this real?

Do you feel played? Sometimes everything seems "normal", but inside we feel we are fighting a weighted heaviness that will not keep us together. Explain yours. When we write in detail some of the stuff we gloss over becomes seen. The best details come in rants or flowing words or in the middle of the night.

~Write or draw your thoughts here~

Interrupt

Lines repeated

Jet forward a demand of obey

Low hung whistling overwhelming the senses. Too overworked they seem to unravel

Filling up

And spouting off with each gust of wind

    Starting and putting out in one breath

Confusion overwhelms the long dead past.

    Little bits of trailing leftovers fill the nostrils with smoky masculine.

    How to rid it, except to not breathe

Pathways set, squish between the toes as if you are taking these steps for the first time.

Trails from nature, ancestors and now found new.

Child knowing, investigating each aspect of the tiny macrocosm of this step.

Are we lost in the now? In the smallness of our sight? Spirit forces us to see beyond. Not as them or us but this hard noise wracking us to our core shaking our very being

How magical is this noise? Breathe it in.

~Write or draw your thoughts here~

"Advanced Exposure"

Cryptic Memories

Unravel from stores of ice house storage melting, molding being left and forgotten

Light house guides travellers

But the ice house keeps the watcher Provided-

Strong, healthy, on guard.

How soon after winter storms can keepers replenish-How many storms can be stayed without replacement of old batteries.

How long does our light need to be protecting us to survive-

Why don't we dive in?

Be part of the ocean rather than warning the surface dwellers of imminent danger ahead

    Just jump in ride the waves

Has my time been wasted in the waiting? Protecting forces seem to need constant attention. This active waiting constructs the fortress of survival.

Who has left you? Who is holding your hand? Are you?

Pain dries out all that have felt it. Our heart wants to feel connection. When we are not feeling we may grab at anything that we bump into. What is beneath the surface? Dive in and feel.

~Write or draw your thoughts here~

"Flicking"

Fresh New Fruit

Cold wash of harshness

Old beggings and new beginnings

Have we held onto the old thinking that it will work if we could just fix it?

Is that the lesson?

Much harder to see that it is broken and unable to be fixed

No way to have it in the new life, the changing life.

    The one that has ease and possibilities

No room for dead weight

    Maybe it doesn't want to be fixed

Can't see it's potential that lies just beyond.

These weights can be unhooked

Choices-

Decisions

    Choosing me comes as a tiny Bud ready to unravel,

take form, unearth from confinement.

      Plucking out old pain is like a death

Grieving is needed but so is hope

So is movement

      Letting go, waiting is anticipation

To see the growth that is fresh and New.

~Write or draw your thoughts here~

Gentle Horizons

Pealing back the gooey layers of distance

Distance between the layers. Striking to the core

Minute forms of fertilizations bring life to hanging clusters of old beauty.

Years of neglect hang rampant on the soul while warm nestling holds onto the old ways.

Finding goodness in last year's model.

    Over extended flexibility causes crackles of joints.

Processing

    Gentle reminders echo pain nattering until we give into, as to not hear the incessant drips of torture

The turn comes in a moment when the drips get too much.

The cut pierces deep and digging around in it can be too painful if we do not give space and gentleness to it.

The explosion can be a shift, a murder, an exhale- an acceptance

We may be both.

Fuzzy creation of, "how it's supposed to be?"

Can keep me wanting

Spine scraping dullness turns beautiful melodies into a black sludge.

-squeaky notices of new building

How much have you grown?

Kari Beyer

~Write or draw your thoughts here~

Falling Down

As I sit here waiting at the stop to take a break

To fill my addiction

to realize that death is waiting alongside me.

Sitting here

Unknown

Smiling, am I just coping?

In five minutes will I know it is?

Is there no need for it?

Am I ready to stand up and walk away?

Kari Beyer

We all have addictions that keep the pain at bay, until we cannot take it any longer. How many times do we look at our phones, tune out, eat, drink, and escape to fill "the void." Thank your body for keeping you safe.

~Write or draw your thoughts here~

"Nourishment"

High Speed Femininity

Scars of forced femininity

Arrangements of backward support curve the edges of selflessness.

The role of support without self-care

How is this working?

A horse shows up

Its role throughout the years has been just that.

But pushing horses hard does not work

For under heavy weighted obligatory horse power help is very strong

self-knowledge of too far

Sometimes missing these hints of warning can cause a push back.

      Can I push to see the raw need for approval, revenge…silent messages to stop?

Take a breath- blown by.

Unforeseen shadows I push by-I can handle the next goal-

Challenge accepted.

If only we were all on the same page

Brain-heart-gut...

My heart strings read a different story

Not always heard from my head

The mushiness of thinking has brought me to fit the normal

    As un-played harp strings beg to be plucked.

Unaware of disjointed melodies being rehearsed on high

    Glimpses of forces needed to pull off the mental feast- while underground happenings pour out in simple carefree easy ways

A forecast does not always march forward without an eye on the scene thermometer

Microscopic changes impact the outcome in gargantuan ways.

Kari Beyer

Knowledge of our faults can be an enormous feat. How do we give gentleness to ourselves to let this connection take place?

~Write or draw your thoughts here~

Hook Handle

Those eyes are a hook handle that pulls me right to the gut

Enveloping my soul

Unlocking a mystery beyond and frequency

has it ever been played

for you.

      The watcher sees the beauty of this moment

sun beating down

Balance that was long fought

A balance that was long fought for

long reached for

stifled by past moments.

Now resolved while looking the other way,

Climbing...

Breathe... wait for it, it is almost here. The ease is needed- wait...

Uncover the passion

The messiness

The overture clicks

The part you need

The shift

The breath-the crowd feels the moment-tingles in the sacrum

Centered-as normal life continues

A diabolical shift just occurred

Observed by you

The song ends with a quiet softness.

Activate - Sometimes these words have no explanation in our mind. We may feel their frequency. When we do not, trust that this is what you need to hear. Close your eyes and take some quiet time for you. Let these words wash over you. When we take time to quiet our thinking and just be with the words, a different type of healing can take place.

~Write or draw your thoughts here~

One Step at a Time

Fields of unforeseen glory-

How quietly they whisper

Gentle wigglings of unseen potential

Because held up high on manmade makings

Set high on delusional glory

While other sets of glory fall so gracefully on fertile soil,

not yet knowing of the place it has found.

Will you be able to root?

      Is there enough space to expand?

Or is it in a place where highways run

Causing annoyance to all that pass by

Why annoyance?

Why not great marketing-

Is survival key?

or is it true and honest grit that nails this glory's roots to the ground?

    A wash of murkiness sends us re-evaluating

gentle folds of clarity wake up the murkiness-

To be evaluated at another time when pain will not be an option-

    The full force of that one needs to be taken in lower doses

One hue at a time

The song is quieting now

Much lighter

Much softer now

Breathe! Feel a shift.

The tightening of support brings a much gentler frequency to be in.

    How easy to be in raindrops of sunlight.

Rather than being pushed to the brink

There seems to be no right time to celebrate. No time to enjoy. No time to be here for yourself. But why? There has always been time for survival, but what if the resting part was just as necessary? The time and space need to be hollowed out. Push aside the boxes and stand here. This is the moment to breathe. Rest here. This is where we expand the space. Practice feeling all emotion.

~Write or draw your thoughts here~

Busy

Busy...
    When we base our life on this
        It becomes dry, messy, cutting, alone
When supported the weight seems easy
    Why not ease?
Expectations- bring us picking up our garbage
        What garbage?-
    It is all treasure
        Left to feel the breeze laid there to
Wear and wain-
    To show its natural beauty with no preconceived notions.
        The nattering can be a beautiful noise
    if you have perspective.
    Felt the trail of life you haven't taken.

Whose path are you living?

    How many interrupting paths have you crossed to make your path?

    What freshly fallen snow have you walked?

        True freshness, has it been not influenced by the sun?

        How do we turn off the noises in our head?

    The busyness that grates our nerves-

        The sounds that only when turned off can the notice of peace become real but only if we observe.

    Getting the head off the real rest

    may take retraining, is it worth it?

        Reverent paths bring tradition

    Tradition is privy to sameness, unchanged

        Even the hippie has tradition of the dress, of the attitude, of the sameness of choice.

        Once found a way that works

        That makes sense

        That we find comfortable

    It is hard to run, hitch, comfort for a whim

        This is why this work is hard, painful and continuous.

~Write or draw your thoughts here~

"Tree of Oneness and Now"

Eradicated Version

Heavy weight held together

by strong straining muscles

Brought on by tightened foot hold

Held in place by pure will

Interrupted by

hopeless vantage points

releases the will to push on

Focus becomes an excuse to muscle through

Whereas the perspective can be altered

to have me looking from weary lenses.

That perspective is sucked into my next breath.

How monumentally over watched am I

Blinded by false networks

      Holding up or hanging onto old fun

is not current enough to truly motivate

Kari Beyer

The illumination is unnecessary
    Ramped up versions of exploitation
    Unveils a mystery that flat lines the desert
    The black cave of survival

THE FREQUENCY OF LIFE

~Write or draw your thoughts here~

Rampant Deforestation

My life has been cluttered with noises, sounds, fullness. Distracting me from my need to hear myself.
My mind keeps going long after signs of fatigue and exhaustion have reared their head. An attitude of-"can't you take it?" challenges me to keep going past the brink. And there is the unsurity and unsecurity of past traumas that have me questioning if I know what is best for me. More distractions. How do I unplug from all of these welcomed old friends? What is making these so important in my life? Is it the distraction that is needed until I am ready to unleash release, the partner that has kept me distracted? To see the main event, the pain, I need to caress, be gentle with, and learn to love myself in another way - a way without need for emotional opinions.
A way of allowance.

Have you taken time today to caress your mind?
~Write or draw your thoughts here~

Hot and Cold

Ring toss on snakehead

Games bring us close to feel childlike

In our venomous games we play

Calculated, dangerous

The reminder of long ago games we used to play

That has stayed with us.

Hot and cold-

Our egos favorite game

That we have kept to play on all occasions.

Emotions running hot

Into the boring freedom of cold

As we are too busy shivering uncontrollably

To appreciate this reprieve.

Hot has us amped up too hot to have rational thought-

Hot under the stress

Overworked ready to blow-

We are too occupied

Our thermostat tells the ego's story, while this disruption has been going on

Our reactionary self-kept busy

Our house remains in disrepair

Life without being the thermostat

Genuine cool cat

Observing the relative moment-

Kari Beyer

~Write or draw your thoughts here~

The Big Picture

generated bliss

Is that truly a thing?

Resolving to halt below the mark

Never measuring up

Floundering in uncharted waters

While sulkily looking backwards at what might have been...

The uncovered Bliss Of the past

that was never realized.

that now looking back seems white washed

with sunlight glowing even though...

through uninterrupted vision sees Black Clouds all around.

reasons of left behind realities never seen through what if eyes.

Obstructed eyes

Prison of the fear of the past has been changed for rose coloured glasses

Kari Beyer

Halting progress of seeing, knowing

Knowing you have made informed decisions

The best decisions for you

at the time of present Easy slopes were never looking like cliffs of slippery Slopes.

at the time I couldn't See the other side

Greener Pastures.

~

There are two meanings in one. The capitalized words give the second message.

Is Resolving Never Floundering

While The Bliss Of Black Clouds

Obstructed

Prison Halting Knowing The Easy Slopes

I See Greener Pastures

What are the double meanings in your life?

~Write or draw your thoughts here~

"Discovery"

Dust Blown

Traditions of changing for survival

Cute puppy-old deformed dog Adapt and survive

Wind whistling by wind worn tree. Adapt and survive

Blending mountain peaks tell the story of adaptation

On a long term scale-

How can hiding the beauty in caves

to preserve youth

be promoting the true scenes

of change.

Movement in growth or preservation of Age-

a moment of time that everything was good.

Is it that or unknowing that made that eagerness for preservation so virile so respected so coveted?

      A time machine wish brings us confronted with new realities.

Remembered memories of hiding yuckies never unveiled before.

    When the Age of mountains have shed with pure force and time,

Blown away like dust.

    Oh to blow those loose thoughts away, dust…

What brighter colours would we see, if we saw the dust right now in its new beauty?

of the present.

Where is our beauty now?

Beauty in the overreaction?

Beauty in the rumbling before the explosion?

Beauty in the little one that has no knowledge, is so innocent? Would you tell them no there is no Beauty in them?

Here…Write.

The Frequency of Life

Dumping Ground

Our intuitive truth

comes from encouragement of speaking the 'truth' or one possible truth.

As I speak this truth.

The double of it being true seeps in.

I want that encouragement to be true.

So I speak it louder.

Louder, to drown out the doubt

To drown out the tests

Is it better to be just the opposite of the negativity? Does this bring healing?

If I concentrate on happy our fears of insignificance, weakness, hatred, war will go away…?

      Has this been working?

If I try a little harder

Have I done enough?

Dumping the guilt into that never ending pit of taking it

What is your heartfelt disappointment?

What would happen if you had no barriers? Could you fulfill your heart? Do you put barriers up between yourself and your heart?

~Write or draw your thoughts here~

Focus Changer

No bird's eye view was offered

Tentacles of stickiness

I was holding on

Pulling tight just to see a sliver of the future

Possibilities.

Generated possibilities that were never opened

Unless that decision was made.

Coming out into the future brought many unforeseen possibilities each one messier than the other.

Has me looking back now

Creating the new messiness of not being in the present

Squishes rooted decisions by becoming too top heavy with heady knowledge of nothingness

Causing dry mouth from not speaking your heart.

What is your present? What is in your present?

~Write or draw your thoughts here~

Self-Speak

Why so hard?

What are the highlights?

Curling around the shape that brings me most joy

The taste of it.

Smell

Of how the sight of it brings me joy

Turning it into that perfect shape it feels beneath my fingers

Curling curving-

The first time without effort-

Thick Petal like-

    Shiny, shimmers

    The landscape opens to blues and greys.

How to describe such delicious flavours

Without the experience of past and present

Knowledge of the unforgiving past

Brings us here to the present-

The moment of unforgiving scenes lingering as a wisp

of a hint that is hard to miss when you sit and think,

but too caught up in the present to really consciously take notice.

The present- Birds singing their song of now-

Not concerned of previous laments

Wind blowing as the sweet smell lifts to let you inhale the beauty.

Is it all for me?

Or am I a quiet observer able to peek into this vast reality?

Kari Beyer

What is for you? Where have you attached to someone else's reality?

~Write or draw your thoughts here~

"Hiding Within"

This is Mine

Locked up tighter than a drum

Waiting for someone to save you

Realizing that you need to be the advocate for yourself

Who holds the key is not the question

Can you get out —out of this jungle not out of your mind?

Out of your mind can be a little stop in between

Waiting in that all too clean waiting room, feeling like the walls are coming in on you.

Thinking...there, there would be the way to live in the waiting room of life, out of your mind.

 As you dive back in you realize it's a jungle.

Our mental health goes hand in hand with our body's health. The mystery is how they go together. How did you get here? Your mind body knows.

~Write or draw your thoughts here~

Circling

The quality of decisions

Layers of beauty

Encapsulated in one choice- one decision

That has been agonized over

Thought about

Dreamt about

Each breath has inhaled stiffly

Shuttering taking in new information

Exhale the harsh edges

Hitting a snag that loops around

unable to exist without outside help

Outside help enters- with veracity

So many opinions on decisions that are not theirs to make

Advise rocking

disappointments internalized

"What ifs" arrive

Pleasing-

Dominating-

Giving up

Swirling on the edge of the flat abyss

That is you.

Wait that is me?

I could go there.

The noise quiets

The ease is here

Of course that is the answer

Hmmmm...

The hum of my body enjoys this moment

Only you know what the right decision is for you. Only you have had your experiences, and only you have been through your traumas. Where are you willing to open?

~Write or draw your thoughts here~

New Directions

Undefinable journey

      Still wet globs of paint

Not locked into dryness-permanency

Able to be watered down,

Smeared into a different shape,

Wiped off and started again,

Transferred,

Or slowly slip off the canvas without much fanfare-

Just a trail letting me know that it was once there

      Not remembered by its beauty that once sat there-

Prominent-

Eye sore swirling mess-

Or beauty in its un-blending,

but just remembered by the stain of interrupted mess that lay in wait for a cover up

 Or an amalgamation to base the whole painting on

What is your life based on? Are the basics of you causing you pain? Is it a constant battle? How is the battle serving you? Give both parts space. The part that needs it and the part that does not.

~Write or draw your thoughts here~

Water Rising

Curious glancer

Closer than is safe. Barely breathing

waiting for an exit

still staying, glancing, pacing.

waiting for the moment to pass.

It doesn't

Staying, waiting

waves radiate wider, larger.

stillness-

no trauma

peace-filled off in the distance

Happiness- only a twinkle

-causing no ripples

movement

but staying with this peace filled moment

Kari Beyer

no running away-

staying power is amazing

What has your soul been through? Have you felt the pain? Have you learned lessons? Been affected?

~Write or draw your thoughts here~

"Dragons"

Generational Journey

Captured by colourful light flares

that exit the Black creature

almost by magic

Entering the realm

with eerie ominous movement

The rampart of existence

furrowed deep within the exit cell

of bubbling emotions

Swirling in this place of loneliness

Thoughts of "I am the only one" alone ness

echoing in these cave walls

The knowledge of the feeling of each

bumpy corridor

Inspection can only bring notice to long hidden judgements

Repeat the act of "newness"

stutter step.

full blown realization

of the stark reality that this is not new

Forlorn shadows of our lives living on repeat.

~Write or draw your thoughts here~

The Old Cold Masculine

      defends, defense
  poppy prickly
winding old cold wood that thrice tried to
go up the new
      But from the weight of growth made new
finds itself looking down intimidating
  The next bright shiny reflection
  Bursting through not opening yet
Wait makes it intolerable
  At the end the old growth is more
noticeable- ready for deflection

Where is the masculine part of you? Where can we welcome our new masculine; the part that balances us - strong, loyal, dominant, fire like, productive, expressive, analytical, outcome based and thoughtful? What does masculine mean to you?

~Write or draw your thoughts here~

Shitty Days

I must be shitty because it looks like shit

These days come around sometimes.

Wandering, looking for their place

No mountain slope can help them slide off easily.

The New growth of you beckons their arrival.

Like an old solid friend that I ask to come in only to realize too late that I feel like shit every time I am around them.

Recognition can misrepresent us pairing it with loyalty and wanting what is best for us, or even knowing us better than we know ourselves.

This pairing has blown past my senses for I have given them away. I am not senseless but for this scenario I am

Unwanted by me

Unhealthy, like a kid who wants to fit in and flings his door open to all.

Fitting in stomps on my barriers; that are now rusted, squashed and unusable.

I pick myself up.

Nothing here for me

Vacating my old home that was so solid and friendly, so I thought.

Rich lathers of the unknown await me, curling through the senses which are now active for me.

Everything is much closer now.

Unknown entities all around keeping me on my toes

Survival as an addict; lost, stolen from, hope

a thing of the past.

Excitement comes- newness and anticipation

Foundations of old barriers have been crumbled. These were not needed. In this destruction we can see where we need to protect our new self. Sometimes family or old friends do not want this change. Our new self needs validation. 1. You have changed! 2. You are healing. 3. You can create your own space. 4. You approve! That is enough. 5. Breathe.

~Write or draw your thoughts here~

Being Elsewhere

Outside wanderings have me hopeful

for getting inside-

  Doors closed tightly, concrete calls

built up to protect, to save

Internal itching's keep me distracted from my goal of getting in.

  Is that why it takes so long?

Or is it because the fortress is fortified to withstand all conscious thought

  Mild protections keep me safe from outside invaders

  While hot anger rips through my body that so badly wants release from.

The cause of anger

Restricted vents of overlapping decay has rot scar Strong edges

Before unhinging the natterings that pull me out again

Kari Beyer

~Write or draw your thoughts here~

Restricted Energies

Overthought exit patterns-no longer working

Captive the presented moment

    Testing is not taken

    Nose in

    keep on pushing.

The entry-not allowed.

    Hand on the back door ready for exit.

Afraid they will get in and see what a mess it is in here

    How raw it is

    Splaying on the floor arms wide open

How can I keep up this pretense?

When I don't know what I am hiding

Know protection is the only key

    Fatigue-tired-from all this rational-

all this work on what is-what do I truly love?

Is that what takes the breath from me?

Makes my nerves tweak with annoying twinges-

helps me concentrate on itching

rather than what I enjoy.

You think that I would be happy to do what I enjoy.

Why does this throw me?

Make me procrastinate?

Have me in my addictions?

    Making the trauma real

How have you pushed past the fear and found your courage?

~Write or draw your thoughts here~

Fun

So disjointed are my wanderings throughout my mind

Uncompared

Sitting waiting

beyond the fear. Fun in the fear?

Cresting above the waves,

Or reverent to the trauma

These two so opposite but right in my face-

Irritation

Why can't either be the way to go?

Not un-attached

but instead I want to taste, feel and smell the trauma

wait in this cold vortex of familiarity because if I play in the fear I may fall off.

Spinning in circles forming barriers that consume me

Or spin in circles in the fear of fun.

Raw anticipation has me falling off again.

Back to play in the waves of uncertainty. While onlookers watch and say, Wow! that looks like fun.

Never participating in that fearless behaviour.

Kari Beyer

How fearless are you right now? What is stopping you from the fun?

~Write or draw your thoughts here~

Protocol of Niceness Part 1

Protocol of Niceness

Fills our weakness

By playing along

What an exit strategy

If I would choose another way

Punishment the only option

Be nice, sit still, shut up

But there lies the silent manipulation

No words are held here

For then there could be some wrong felt.

Cold hearted manipulation in the form of the loving feminine not easily noticed

Silent desperate survival

Who could see the boundary crossed?

As mother slips by the security guard with easy innocence

Playing along the only option

Because if angered years of wrath may smite you for upsetting

Such a little old 'vulnerable' innocence

Such futile strength is held in the lamb.

One not easily fought

And less likely to have won.

~Write or draw your thoughts here~

"Much More Balance"

The Protocol of Niceness Part 2

This battle is the one we fight ourselves every day-

one may say only mothers and daughters,

but no

so much more subtle is the war that rages between mothers and their sons.

So quiet

So unexpected

Sons have no idea of the battle, only that they have to take care of their sweet mother

Protecting the enemy

Kari Beyer

How is your relationship with the masculine part of you?

What is your relationship with the feminine part of you?

~Write or draw your thoughts here~

Three Thoughts to Hope

1

The comparative norm

Does this lead to deep satisfaction?

Brain turned off

clicking in the "I can do it" attitude.

Encouragement ringing in my ears

staying close to the hand that feeds.

Failing not an option

Waiting protectors

Sit on edge or fall into uncharted territory.

Fear will bring you back to mid ground, in the beginning.

This is considered protection.

To teach, to control, to explore- but not too much

More about knowing limits.

Unlimited is not an option

to let me know there is hope.

But like all things hope is just the encouragement I need to

"make something of myself"

Strive for better

How limitless am I actually?

This pre-pubescent training, is it real?

2

Gathering sawdust

Folding over

Tight corners

Marking the area to hold in the tight filled

Stuffing packed membrane

That only the silent ripples can penetrate.

Keeping distractedly holding on

Only realizing later on that the sharks are herbivores.

That all will be safe

Letting go of the sawdust can leave me free to receive

Other goodness without tight corners

3

Looking for the entry point

Narrowed down to one point, immunity

Flapping in the bushes

Does not leave much room to lift off

Balconies leave room. I have to find the one that is right for me.

Without being pulled back.

ripples starting on all points releasing re-connecting-

the stillness matters.

Bringing a realignment in the universe of time and dispatch weaving a complicated pattern

that pattern that is acceptable for your whole

a pattern that has been danced before

a sacred pattern that is watched over

and needed for me today to release

re-still my lines of energy to capture my soul.

To bring it down to the dust

and let me remember my origin of purity.

How do you see you?

Can you see the times you have "fallen" with love and gentleness? Your best life is here; not having so many opinions on different subjects. There is a choice that is best for you in each moment. Give yourself the room to make choices each time and feel what is right for you. If your body disagrees with you it is a lesson to learn and you were not ready until now. Your body will give you clues.

Who are you?

Do you need to answer?

Breathe in and out love.

~Write or draw your thoughts here~

"Heart of A Woman"

Epilogue

Registering softly for a voice to fill the atmosphere

Funnelling down my center —introspection down not receiving

Release point furtive way

Creating a repeated pattern that lulls the release to remember its ways

Wings fluttering- making sounds of crispness- like waves hitting the shore

Hitting the shores of newness

Washing over old similar places to bring new information to cross that line to hope

Hope as a reality this time.

Not un-promised or abandoned,

something real and un-hesitated.

It comes in the gentle breeze like ease rolling in the soul.

Like tiredness leaving, melting off

receiving peace without any switch being turned.

It just is.

Leaving the wrapped notions behind

That would help me <u>exist</u>

And I do

Seeing that long line that has brought me here

Seeing it brings me peace of my history

like an old woman pleased to look back with satisfaction of the tale.

Kari Beyer

How do we step into hope in the present and be abundance rather than keep it out of our reach?

~Write or draw your thoughts here~

Uncovering

Distraction after distraction avail themselves

Helping me to avoid the heart peace moment

Words escape me

To explain the tapestry that lay beneath

The uncovering- that if unfocused can be forgotten

Until it is available to be sought after next time

And this is a heart focusing.

Woven patterns cannot be logically traced back by the mind

In the inches of blankness come the peace that surrounds-

With fluttering rejection

The survival kicks in when we need it

And sometimes when we don't

How do we feed the peace?

Long quieted by necessary survival.

Kari Beyer

~Write or draw your thoughts here~

Who I Am

Hot yellow scars of healing

Pulsating vibrant energy

Across non-existent scales of black

Uncovering familiar feelings

That breathed in has me exhaling

Even though the breath was not finished

Interrupted

Now laying horizontal

Weighted down by heavy loads of

Heart felt pain

Expelling has the scent outside,

Unable to inhale again

    Ridding self of stench

    Many tries, unsuccessful

    What does this scent of pain bring up?

On first breath, automatic repulse

But second is more forgiving? No

    More like some awoken scent receptor, turned off for a second smell.

Third smell has them all turned off forgotten

Rejected so that memory filled scents can no longer awaken the pain

Who are you now? Close your eyes and feel that question. It may not be ready for words. It may be an emotion, a feeling, or a sound. Celebrate this knowledge of you.

~Write or draw your thoughts here~

"Finite Wonder"

Personal

These are some examples about how I use the word art and artwork. This is an opportunity to tell our stories to heal. Sometimes our stories get told over and over again. Whether you tell friend, family member or repeat them to yourself. Stories become anchored into us on a physical, emotional and mental level. This work is about telling the stories to let go. See your stories in a new light and learn from them. Heal from them. Do the shaking and release the old traumas.

Mom and Me

Relationships are where I start, mothers, friends, acquaintances, fathers, siblings and the relationship with myself. For me the turning point was the relationship with my mother that helped me open my heart wisdom.

"Muscles atrophied from many years of paralyzed muscles. Closed open hand."

My mother had a stroke over 12 years ago.

There have been many stages I have gone through. The one thing I am most grateful for is that the stroke has left her relatively in silence. For the majority of her life she has been a talker, but in her silence I have gained the space and time to find out who I am. At first the silence was deafening. She left a hole where her voice normally was. More than that, the voice in my head that her talking would regularly drown out was in my face. I got angry. I busied myself with many things. Tried to take care of her, get her better, fight her fight, or fight anyone else's fight, but mine. A lot of blame had lived in these hallways. As much as I was blaming her for so many things the voices in my head were mostly about me, devastating to me. This is where the real work was.

I talked to my mom about loving herself one day. She did not know what that meant. I can see now where I started my journey; I did not know what loving myself looked like. I was so consumed by all the talk and loud voices in my head that the concept of quiet was foreign.

How did I teach my daughters, and son? I know my mom has loved. She loved us her children, even though I was constantly questioning that. She didn't live up to my standards. But where did I get those standards? Does my mom constantly question herself? How much room do I need to be able to hear the wisdom of my own heart?

Changing our frequencies opens our hearts to new paths. Turning off the voices in our heads and feeling our heart's wisdom. Sitting in my heart's silence has helped me to acknowledge my role in this mother-daughter relationship that I have helped to create. In seeing this I have been able to heal and create a new relationship with my mom. She has allowed me to be able to heal without her input. I don't think this would have happened without her silence. In this silence my mom has been in her body mind more. She has expressed her emotions through her art just as I do.

How does this lesson pertain to me? There is allowance of healing in the silence, something that helps my journey and the journey of others around me. There is no forcing the healing. The healing comes for everyone differently. The thing about silence is that it is a double edged sword; it can create space or take up space. It is our decision what we do with that space.

"Mounting Blue"

These are the words that I have to describe the painting, unedited:

A long walk

Lines crossed, path crossed

Ridges of blue

Either wind pushing

Waves falling off

Bunched up

Bear

Hesitation

God looking down, hooded creature

White all around

Yellow-green blobs

This is what is going on in my life right now: I feel that I am riding a wave with white foam all around me lifting me up. I looked up the "Bear" meaning. What stands out for me is courage! Fear yes but doing it anyway. Support is the other word for "Bear" and I feel I have the support in the people around me. Also I feel that I can give myself support. "Ridges of blue" is about speaking my truth. Writing this book! "Lines crossed, path crossed" is my hesitation and changes that are going on in my life. "God looking down" on me and the "hooded creature" is about duality in my life, limiting beliefs. "Green-yellow" blobs are about my heart. I feel that there is more here. I think we will see how this unfolds!! So interesting, I wrote yellow-green up top and green-yellow down below. Our mind likes to mess with us. It has a habit of protecting us from painful memories, sometimes this can be an entire memory or it can be simple, like switching a word (yellow-green to green-yellow) around so it doesn't have the same meaning. No wonder I could go no further.

As I breathe with this painting I feel different sensations in my body. My jaw is tingling and I cannot sit still. I also am struggling to just observe and not judge myself for choosing one aspect over another. All these observations are from different parts of my life. They come together because they need to be observed together. They all live in different places of my body mind. In observing this painting it lets my body tell the story.

Now for the hard part! No judgements or making the stories more than they are. Now breathe!! I feel that I need to breathe into my heart. The other thing is to bring the words I wrote and the painting into my heart and let it be there while I breathe.

Sexy

My husband said to me last night that I was sexy. I said, "You think I am sexy?" to make sure I understood correctly. He said, "Yes I do- and you think you're sexy." I said, "How do you know that?" He said, "Even when you were thinner you did not dance in the mirror or to me like you do now."

Wow!!

This has me thinking of all the pictures of me when I was thinner. I remember those days when I would scold myself for my hips being too big or tummy. Those pictures I look at today 5, 10, 20 years later and I see how perfect I was. What was I thinking? The internal scolding has been quieter now. Some have disappeared. I am able to allow myself to be sexy, truly.

"Satisfied"

Some words that I would use to describe this painting:

Drippy dullness

Cold aching pains

A thin line in the distance

Streaky

Wispy

Standing out dullness

Escaped blobs

Big ridges

This is an interesting painting. I liked painting it because I chose my composition and it was came together so quickly and easily. "People thought it was amazing so I stopped painting." This statement is the key for me. Then another thought pops in my head. The other day we were having a discussion about how some people go all in. If they are excited about a certain thing they will consume themselves with it. I have not done this for myself and if I have, I have quit if there is any positive feedback. I feel these two attitudes are connected to this limiting belief I have had about praise and hiding myself. The title is interesting too. As I wrote "Satisfied" it bothered me. What is satisfied? Don't I want more than just being satisfied? How can I be satisfied in the dullness?

As I look back at my words that I wrote I can see how they

describe my attitude not only to the painting but in life. This is a different way to look at the words. Describe how you feel when you are painting, running, observing, or any of the 'ing' words. Rant about them. This is where you get your best material. Your barriers are down and you can say what you mean. Leave it open if you can handle it, see what is next, if not, book a healing session and see where that guides you.

Loving Me

I had a dream about my Aunt and her mom. Her mom and I were walking in this museum café. We were visiting and having a nice time- My Aunt was there. She was younger and thinner than when she passed away. She was holding her arms out. I ran to hug her. I told her that I loved her. I don't think I ever did that. After I woke, the feeling never passed. She was so vibrant. Her mom was happy. The feeling of joy all around me was intense.

How long do we have to wait to loosen the chains of propriety so we can give ourselves that "open hug of honesty" and revel our feelings.

What joy

To feel that beauty

Deep beauty

Around you

The feeling in the dream was not a thing I shared with my

aunt. We did not express our love openly. More to the point this was my dream, how do I express my love to others? Do they know what my feelings are? Do I hold those feelings in because of many different excuses? Are these excuses holding me back from love?

How can I open my expression of my heart? How can I trust to not trample my own spirit and lead myself to a deeper understanding of who I am?

Some of our healing leads us to more questions than answers. If we are able to sit with these questions not necessarily to find the yes/no answers but to trust that something greater will answer, the answers can come organically and in ways that we could not imagine. Let go of the reigns and fly.

ABOUT THE AUTHOR

Kari Beyer has lived most of her life in Saskatchewan but her early years were spent on the west coast of Canada. Spending those key years by the ocean, Kari is always drawn to water, swimming, and being at the lake as much as possible. On a quest to always dig deeper, whether it be in conversation, healing, or understanding, Kari is finding the balance and allowance as an artist, writer, mother, wife, and grandmother. Kari lives and runs Kari's Healing Space in Saskatoon, SK.

For more information about Kari and her work visit:

www.karishealingspace.com

INDEX

There is no index in this book because the words and art are left for your own interpretation. Open yourself to your own meanings.

www.ingramcontent.com/pod-product-compliance
Lightning Source LLC
Chambersburg PA
CBHW061208070526
44583CB00025B/3156